THE BEAUTIFUL MATANUSKA VALLEY

All photographs in this book, unless indicated otherwise, are by the author, Helen Hegener.
Complete notes on photographs and images can be found on page 136.

Hegener, Helen
    The Beautiful Matanuska Valley / Helen Hegener
    ISBN (ISBN) 978-0-9843977-5-4 (0-9843977-5-2)
1. Alaska 2. Alaska ~ Pictorial works
Includes appendixes, maps, resource listing, index

To order single copies of this book send $29.95 (plus $5.00 shipping) to:
Northern Light Media, PO Box 298023, Wasilla, Alaska 99629-8023
To order this book online visit http://northernlightmedia.com
Please make PayPal payments to helenhegener@gmail.com
Please support independent booksellers by ordering through your local independent bookstore.
Also available at Amazon, eBay, and wherever good books are sold.

Wholesale orders welcome, bulk orders and special purchases available. Contact us for details.

http://northernlightmedia.com

4

To the memory of my parents, Bill and Virginia Fikes, who brought

us to this beautiful valley so long ago because they believed it would be a

good place to raise their family, and they were right, and now their

great-grandchildren are raising families here.

~ ~ ~ ~ ~

"This valley is just a little piece of heaven.

Everything I ever hoped to find is here."

James Landehorne, 1948

Preface

I first saw the Matanuska Valley in August of 1965, when we rolled through it on our way to my father's new post assignment at Fort Richardson, 40 miles south. There were many later trips out to 'the Valley,' as it was referred to, because my parents loved the expansive views of farms, lakes, mountains and rivers, and as they got to know a few people who lived in the Valley, we visited as often as possible.

I recall a trip we made north through the Valley in 1966, to the end of the gravel road near Talkeetna. Many years later I would travel that same road twice a week, helping my friend Margaret Heaven deliver the mail to Big Lake, Willow, and all points north of Wasilla. In the early 1970's there were so few people living north and west of Wasilla that we could deliver all their mail in one day and only needed to do it twice weekly.

That all started changing after the oil pipeline. The roads were paved, the farms were subdivided, big box stores and fast food places sprouted seemingly overnight, and it felt like every time we turned around another stoplight was going in somewhere in the Valley.

Times changed, and we changed with them. My parents are buried on Fort Richardson now, but their great-grandchildren are growing up in this Valley, and the beauties which drew my parents here, the things they loved most about this place, the mountains, lakes, rivers, beautiful views and friendly people, are all still here. Every time I look up at the mountains which tower over this Valley, or admire a lake or a scenic view, I whisper a 'thank you' to them for making this Great Land - and this great valley - our family's home so long ago.

~ Helen Hegener

Introduction

The Trails Became Highways

The Matanuska Valley is vibrantly rich in history. There are still remnants of the early trails winding across the Valley and into the mountains, game trails which were first used by Native hunters and families, and then later by explorers, miners, trappers, and others seeking access into or passage through the forbidding terrain which surrounds the Matanuska Valley on three sides.

Today's Glenn Highway winds through some of the most geologically spectacular land in Alaska: the Matanuska River Valley, carved over centuries by the 27-mile long glacier which gives the river and the Valley their melodic name.

South, East, North, West . . .

This book is organized into six parts: South, East, North, West, Palmer, and Wasilla. The compass delineations are not precise, and there were some tough decisions about what to include and what simply wouldn't fit.

The intention was to divide this somewhat unwieldy subject into identifiable and easily digestible parts, while maintaining the integrity and clarity of the whole. My goal was to make a little of the history accessible and interesting, and to make the tremendous diversity and variety of the Matanuska Valley understandable.

A Place to Begin

This volume is by no means a comprehensive book, but merely an introduction to the many wonders and delights of this place. My hope is that it will provide a good start for exploring on your own.

Whether this is your first visit to the beautiful Matanuska Valley or you've lived here for many years, my hope is that I've succeeded in providing a greater understanding and a new appreciation for this amazing place we call home.

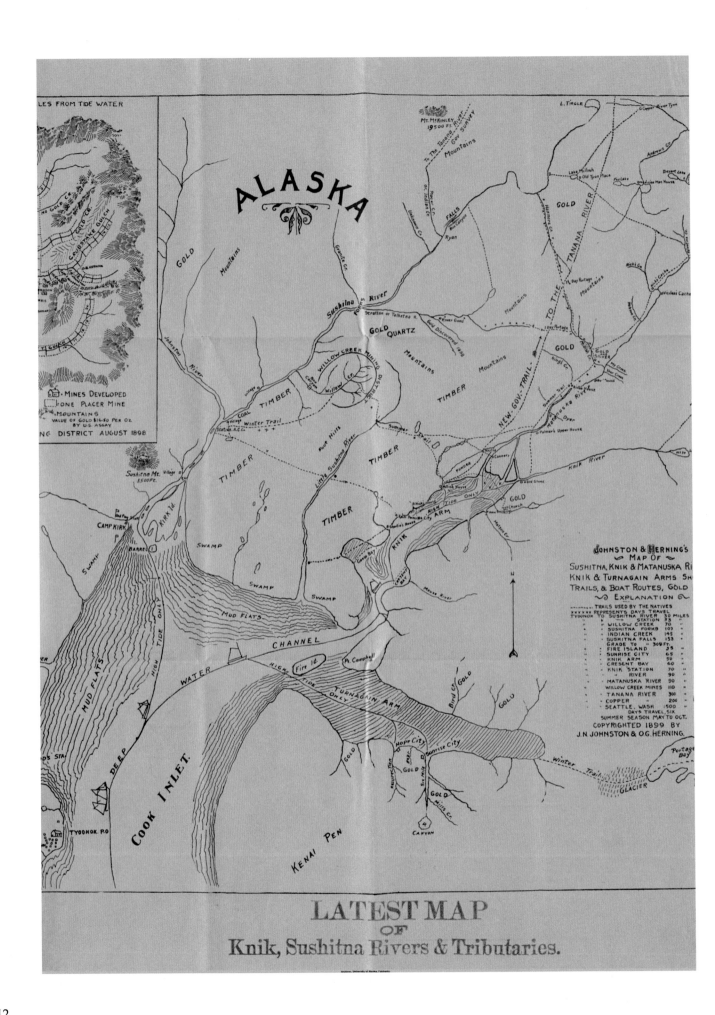

LATEST MAP
OF
Knik, Sushitna Rivers & Tributaries.

12

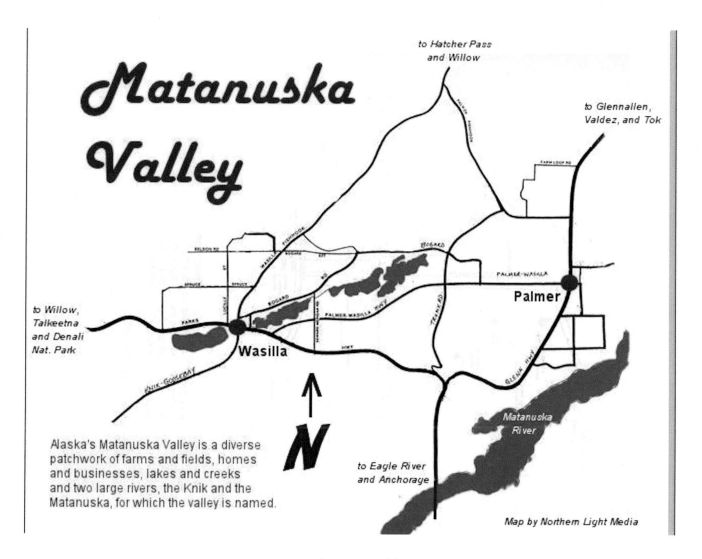

Alaska's Matanuska Valley is a diverse patchwork of farms and fields, homes and businesses, lakes and creeks and two large rivers, the Knik and the Matanuska, for which the valley is named.

Map by Northern Light Media

Matanuska Valley Maps

Maps are plentiful in the Valley

The earliest maps of the Matanuska Valley were undoubtedly drawn in the dirt with a stick, as a hunter described where he saw a moose or a fisherman explained where he caught a brightly shining salmon. Later maps may have been drawn on the tanned hides of animals, and much later there were sketchings on paper leading to the gold discoveries and routes to and from the sparse settlements of pioneers.

Today the Matanuska Valley is filled with maps showing details of history, geography, geology, and more, and up-to-date printed maps are readily available at the many visitor centers scattered throughout the Valley.

Maps are even found online via computer or cellphone; simply search for the name of a location or a landmark and a profusion of excellent maps will appear, with descriptions and photographs and helpful reviews of whatever local attractions can be found in the vicinity.

Part One ~ South

Point Mackenzie to the Knik Glacier

The southern edge of the Matanuska Valley is sharply defined by water and vertical land: The Knik River, which flows out of the Knik Glacier and into Knik Arm, and Pioneer Peak and the Chugach Mountains, rising almost straight off the water in an impressive show of soaring altitude.

Pioneer Peak, right, towers over the Wes Grover farm, with three Matanuska Colony barns dating from 1936. The great peak soars over Bodenburg Butte, the Knik and Matanuska RIvers, and the entire Matanuska Valley, dominating the southern skyline, and it's iconic image is found on many local business logos. The photo above shows sled dog musher and Iditarod founder Joe Redington Sr.'s famous wooden fishing boat, the *Nomad,* where it has been resting for decades, on the mudflats at Knik, with the waters of Knik Arm close behind it. The small photo at right is a Siberian Iris, a common wildflower which blooms in many marshy areas of the Valley in springtime.

Knik Arm

Only a river . . .

Knik Arm is the northernmost branch of Cook Inlet, a great body of water which stretches 180 miles from the Gulf of Alaska and splits at Anchorage into Knik Arm and the more southern Turnagain Arm.

William Bligh, who served as Captain Cook's Sailing Master on his third and final voyage, thought that both Knik Arm and Turnagain Arm were the mouths of rivers and not the opening to the Northwest Passage.

Under Cook's orders Bligh organized a party to travel up Knik Arm, and they quickly returned to report that Knik Arm indeed led only to a river.

Boats of any kind are a rare sight on Knik Arm today, but in times long past the Arm was traversed by rowboats, freighters, and sailing ships. George Palmer, a merchant who owned stores in Knik and near the later site of Palmer, frequently crossed the Knik Arm, as cited here by Valley historian Colleen Mielke: "Palmer's first schooner, the two masted 'C. T. Hill,' arrived at Knik Harbor June 7, 1913. Leaving his store in the hands of a clerk, Palmer and crew sailed the schooner from Goose Bay to San Francisco, two or three times a summer and brought back merchandise for his store." And: "In the spring of 1915, Palmer traveled to Seward, by dog sled, where he boarded a steamer to San Francisco to purchase a newer schooner named 'The Lucy.' Palmer and 'The Lucy' arrived at Goose Bay on May 3, 1915."

Colleen Mielke later reports: "A fearless boatman, Palmer made routine trips from Knik to Tyonek, Sunrise, Hope and Seldovia, bucking the relentless Turnagain Arm wind and tide, in a small open gas boat."

horses grazing on excellent pasture on the Fla...

Palmer Hay Flats

Vast Natural Grazing Lands

Farmers who homesteaded the Matanuska Valley in the early years of the nineteenth century found natural grazing lands for their cattle, sheep, and horses in the flat lands between the last wooded bluffs and the channels of Knik Arm. Dubbed the Palmer Hay Flats, these wide open pastures were a welcome sight to the later farmers who arrived with the 1935 Matanuska Colony Project with cattle and horses to feed.

Good Friday Earthquake

On March 27th, 1964, a 9.2 earthquake changed the nature of the Palmer Hay Flats forever, lowering the ground by a couple of feet in some areas, much more in others.

What had been dry pasture-like hayfields became marshy swampland, and skeletal ghost forests, a result of the subsidence of the land which occurred during the Good Friday earthquake, still stand in many areas.

Today the former grazing lands are a birder's paradise, hosting thousands of migratory waterfowl each year.

Palmer Hay Flats Game Refuge

The vast expanse of the Palmer Hay Flats State Game Refuge, one of six refuges managed by the Palmer Fish and Game office, is a unique and increasingly accessible place, with trails for wildlife viewing and shelters for family gatherings. The Cottonwood Creek and Reflections Lake sites are the first to be developed, with trails and facilities for visitors. Community outreach events and programs connect people with the land through recreation and education, and eventually a year round nature, science, and public use facility will be available for learning about the wonders of wetland ecosystems, migrating birds, and the seasonal ebb and flow of wildlife.

Knik

The original village of Knik, from a Tainana word meaning 'fire,' developed during the gold rushes between 1898 and 1916. Listed on the 1880 US census, the town of 'Kinik' was populated by Athabaskan Indians, known as Dena'ina. George W. Palmer, the first permanent white resident of the Matanuska Valley, befriended the Dena'ina and lived with them as he developed the first privately owned stores in the Valley.

In 1900 Orville G. Herning arrived in Knik, by which time the white population had risen to 100. Herning was hired to open a trail to the Willow Creek Mining District, and by 1905 Knik had a post office, two stores, a roadhouse and several cabins. In an article titled "Seward Trail for Winter Route," the *Iditarod Pioneer* reported on August 10, 1910: "From the mouth of the Yentna to Seward the trail will be traveled all winter and many roadhouses are located at convenient distances. The Susitna Station is quite a new town where the A.C. Co. has a large store and supplies can be had. Then the trail passes by Knik, another town and post office where there are three restaurants and two good stores..."

By 1915, the peak year for the town, around 500 people lived in Knik, and there were four general stores, four hotels, three saloons, a fuel company, a movie house, barber shop and pool room, and a newspaper, *The Knik News*. When the federal railroad chose to route their line about 15 miles north of Knik, through the area which later became Wasilla, the businesspeople of Knik moved to the new trading center and the town of Knik began fading into history. Today only two original buildings remain: the Pool Hall, which now houses the Knik Museum, and the Bjorn Cabin. The Knik townsite was listed on the National Register of Historic Places in 1973.

Old Knik

Above: *Three dogsled teams at Knik, March, 1920. The mushers are Irving Reed, George Glass, and his son Ophir Glass. They began a trip on the Iditarod Trail from Wasilla. In a magazine article, "Rainy Pass by Dog Team" Reed wrote, "George had modestly set our first overnight stop at the town of Knik, fourteen miles from Wasilla. Knik was still the main gateway on the coast for travel to the Innoko and Iditarod gold fields, with a hotel and large restaurant..." (Alaska Sportsman, Oct. 1965). [Reed Family Papers, UAF-1968-21-214] The Iditarod Trail, opened in 1911 by the Federal Government for the delivery of mail from Seward to Nome, passed through Knik, making it an important supply and transfer point.*

Opposite: *Main Street, Knik, 1914.*

Left: *Knik Pier, 1898. This site was first inhabited by the Dena'ina peoples. The first white resident, George Palmer, lived among the Dena'ina and was the agent for a small trading post of the Alaska Commercial Company. An excellent history of the Knik area can be found online at Coleen Mielke's website: http://freepages.genealogy.rootsweb.ancestry.com/~coleen/knik.html*

KNIK, ALASKA.

Point Mackenzie

A View to the Future

The photo on the opposite page is a view across one of the many hayfields at Point Mackenzie, toward the southeast and the distant Chugach Range above Anchorage and Eagle RIver. Knik Arm is between the point and those mountains. The still relatively undeveloped Point Mackenzie area has been the target of oversized dreams for many years, including a domed city and a bridge across Knik Arm to Anchorage.

Point Mackenzie Dairy Project

The 14,000 acre Point MacKenzie Dairy Project, begun in 1982, was comprised of land which the State of Alaska sold to private individuals, in a lottery, below market value, for the development of dairy farms. The farmers were eligible for loans up to $2.4 million each to develop the farms, but they contracted to develop the land based on a schedule set by the State, which included provisions such as limiting each farm to 50 cows and requiring production within three years. A number of farmers sued the State over the untenable situation, but only eight of the farms ever made it into production, and by 1991, all of the farms had failed, doomed by a State imposed design that was not economically well-constructed.

Railroad Extension to Houston

Currently under construction is a 35-mile rail line to connect the Port of Point Mackenzie, the closest deepwater port to the interior of Alaska, to the existing Alaska Railroad near Houston, which will make the development of natural resources in interior Alaska more economically feasible, and will generate future development of the Point Mackenzie area.

Pioneer Peak

A major peak in the Chugach mountain range, Pioneer Peak is the most prominent landmark in the Matanuska Valley, rising 6,398 feet over the sea-level Knik River. Named in 1939 to honor the hardworking settlers who called the Matanuska Valley their home, Pioneer Peak's iconic profile can be found on business logos around the Valley.

According to *Shem Pete's Alaska*, the Dena'ina people called the mountain *Dnal'iy* or *Denal'iy*, meaning 'The Object That Is Standing Still,' or 'The One That Watches Us.' Contributor Mike Theodore noted, "They say it is a bear's face watching us."

A popular hiking destination, the Pioneer Ridge-Austin Helmers Trail climbs the eastern shoulder of the mountain, starting barely 200 feet off the river and ascending steeply to the southern summit by traversing the northeast slope of the mountain.

Reflections Lake

Named for the spectacular views

Reflections Lake is a quiet wayside near the confluence of the Knik and Matanuska Rivers, offering an easy mile-long walk around the lake. An informational kiosk and interpretive panels at the trailhead help to orient visitors and explain the diversity of seasonal animals which can often be seen, including swans, ducks, geese, loons, beaver, muskrats, hares and moose. The lakeside path offers spectacular views of the Chugach Mountain peaks, bridges, benches, and a section of boardwalk across an interesting wetland section.

The path around the lake passes through birch, cottonwood and alders, which host many songbirds from spring through summer. Colorful wildflowers are abundant, especially in June and early summer. Reflections of the nearby mountains, source of the lake's name, can be spectacular when the water is not frozen over, but when the frost sets in, winter skiing, snowshoeing and ice skating make this area a winter wonderland.

Mile 30.6, Glenn Highway

The Reflections Lake wayside is reached via off ramps at mile 30.6 on the Glenn Highway, just north of the Knik River bridge. Just past the wayside, the road dead-ends at the Knik River, providing access to the river for experienced boaters. *Note: due to changing tide levels, strong river currents, high winds and numerous navigation hazards including submerged gravel bars, only experienced boaters with local knowledge should attempt to operate boats on the Knik River.*

Eklutna Power Plants

Early Electrification of Anchorage

Frank I. Reed founded the Anchorage Light & Power Company in 1923 and developed the Eklutna Power Plant, harnessing the power of the Eklutna River in 1929. A concrete arch dam, 98 feet long and 61 feet high, diverted water from the Eklutna River and into an 1,800 foot tunnel through Goat Mountain, to the concrete powerhouse. The Old Eklutna Power Plant provided 2,000 kW of power, during which time the city grew from a small railroad settlement into the largest city in Alaska. In an era dominated by federal projects, Frank Reed built an independent power company which supplied the city of Anchorage for over 25 years. Reed sold his power plant to the city for $1,000,000 in 1943. When the New Eklutna Power Project was authorized in 1950, the old Eklutna plant was shut down and the dam allowed to fill with silt and gravel. The powerhouse is listed on the National Register of Historic Places.

The New Eklutna Power Project

The New Eklutna Power Project, funded and built by the Department of the Interior's Bureau of Reclamation, was built several miles upriver from the old power plant. A 4.5 mile long tunnel was bored through East Twin Peak to provide water for the New Eklutna Power Plant. Drilling the nine foot diameter tunnel from both the Knik River side and the Eklutna Lake side began in 1951 and connected in October, 1953 - a marvelous engineering feat for its day. The Eklutna Project was dedicated on August 29, 1955, providing a 33,000 kW capacity to the city of Anchorage, the military bases of Fort Richardson and Elmendorf, and communities in the Matanuska-Susitna Borough.

Knik River

A Rouche Moutonee

The photo above show a great rock outcrop, a familiar sight to motorists and part of the Eklutna Tribal Lands. Known as Knik Knob, it sits beside the Knik River, next to the Glenn Highway bridge over the river. Geologists identify this large rock outcropping as a 'rouche moutonee,' or 'plucked hill,' which is a rock formation created by the wearing actions of an ancient glacier passing over it.

The Knik River begins at the Knik Glacier, deep in the Chugach Mountains, and weaves a braided path down the Knik River Valley before consolidating itself as it rounds Pioneer Peak, meets a channel of the Matanuska River, and empties into the Knik Arm branch of Cook Inlet. Knik River sunset photo courtesy of Robert Lutz.

Knik River Road

A drive up the Knik River Road begins at the parallel bridges crossing the river, the first bridge, a beautiful multi-span construction, was completed in 1937 (above), and the sturdy concrete replacement which is used today, finished in 1972. The road skirts the northern boundary of Chugach State Park, following the river along the edge of massive Pioneer Peak and up the valley carved by Knik Glacier. Stellar views of the river, the huge Knik Glacier, and the southern edge of Marcus Baker Glacier, high to the left of Knik Glacier, make this drive an enjoyable afternoon's outing, and in the fall it is an excellent berry-picking area.

There are multiple places to enjoy the Knik River, from a walk across the now-abandoned old Knik River Bridge to a stop at what's locally called the Swimming Hole, a large gravel bar on a bend in the river which is a popular picnic spot in summer. In fall and winter it becomes a favorite gathering place from which to watch and photograph the northern lights over the mountains east of Palmer.

Knik Glacier

The Glacier at the Head of the Valley

The Knik Glacier is 25 milies long and over five miles wide, one of the largest icefields in southcentral Alaska, and one of 18 National Natural Landmarks in Alaska. The glacier feeds the 25-mile long Knik River, which empties into Knik Arm. The Knik Glacier, like the Matanuska Glacier and the many smaller glaciers visible on the surrounding mountains, is a remnant of the tremendous ice field which once covered the entire Valley and created its hundreds of lakes and several significant landforms such as Knik Knob, Bodenburg Butte, and the Crevasse Moraine area.

Knik Glacier and Valley History

The Knik Glacier played a significant role in the history of the Matanuska Valley, as it was responsible for an unusual annual event which directly affected towns and settlers in the Valley. Behind the Knik Glacier is Lake George, a rare geological phenomenon known as a "jokulhlaup" (an ice dammed lake) or self-dumping lake. Over millennia the lake carved a deep gorge down the southern edge of the Knik Glacier, and each year the glacier would advance and block the outflow, and when the spring melt raised the water level in the lake, it would suddenly 'dump' millions of gallons of water and ice into the Knik River. This annual flooding created havoc for the early Native villages, and the later towns and farms along the river. Inexplicably, 1967, after the 1964 Good Friday Earthquake, the self-dumping action stopped.

Knik Glacier is only accessible by boat, helicopter, or all-terrain vehicle. Local adventure companies offer tours via all three modes of transportation.

Part Two ~ East

Bodenburg Butte to the Matanuska Glacier

The eastern side of the Matanuska Valley is a magnificent panorama of rugged mountains, huge river valleys, and broad glaciers which can be seen from high points in almost every part of the Valley.

Another defining characteristic of the eastern side of the Valley is the large number of picturesque farms and homesteads, many of which are the direct result of the 1935 Matanuska Colony Project. The photo on the opposite page shows the Doc McKinley Colony barn, south of Palmer. The iconic Colony barns can be seen in many areas, but several are easily seen along the Springer Loop area south of Palmer. Today's farmers are continuing to tend the land and produce prize-winning vegetables, as well as fresh produce for local stores and farmer's markets. Wild honey, beautiful flowers, dairy products and much more make the Palmer area an agricultural showplace for Alaska.

Matanuska River

The Dividing River

The Matanuska River, which tumbles out from underneath the glacier of the same name, winds between the coastal Chugach Mountains to the south and the interior Talkeetna Range to the north, providing a clear delineation between the two. The Matanuska River valley was traveled extensively by the early Athabascan Indians, and the Matanuska River country was a traditional center of trade between indigenous peoples of the northern, or interior, lands, and the more southern areas around Cook Inlet. According to Wikipedia, "the indigenous Dena'ina Athabascan name for the rive river is Ch'atanhtnu, based on the root -tanh 'trail extends out', meaning literally 'trail comes out river'. The English place name Matanuska derives from the Dena'ina 'Ch'atanhtnu Li'a', referring to the Matanuska Glacier. Li'a is the Dena'ina word for 'glacier' or 'ice'."

Talkeetna Mountain Hadrosaur

Many fine fossils have been discovered in the Matanuska Formation on the north side of the Glenn Highway, including the bones of a dinosaur known as the 'Talkeetna Mountain Hadrosaur,' the first known occurrence of a hadrosaur in southcentral Alaska. The Glenn Highway, named for an early explorer of the route, is one of three national scenic byways in Alaska. Mountain peaks so numerous that many remain unnamed, deep river valleys, canyons, creeks, waterfalls, glaciers... For 75 miles the river braids its way along the valley floor, inaccessible for most of the route, but providing an unforgettably scenic panorama for travelers on the Glenn Highway, which roughly parallels the river for its entire course.

Bodenburg Butte

The Last Shaman of the Eklutna

Bodenburg Butte has been a Valley landmark since pre-historic times... The Athapaskan Dena'ina Indians traveled through the area on a winter trail from Old Knik (Eklutna) to the Knik River, to the Matanuska River and up to the Copper River. According to James Kari, University of Alaska Fairbanks, there was a large Dena'ina village called 'Hutnaynut'i,' or 'Burnt Over,' in the Bodenburg area, where Alex Vasily (Eklutna Alex) was born, the last shaman of the Eklutna Dena'ina."

John Bodenburg and Victor Falk

John Bodenburg took out the first homestead, on the northeast side of the Butte, in 1917, bravely fording the mighty Matanuska River with his small herd of cattle. After he died his farm was purchased by Victor Falk, for whom Falk Lake and Falk Road are named. A slowly deteriorating log barn is all that remains of the Bodenburg homestead.

1935 Colony Barns

In 1935 the Matanuska Colony Project brought new families to the Butte area, as most of the south and east sides were included in the lottery-drawn tracts of farmland. Several of the distinctive Colony barns can be seen on a drive around Bodenburg Loop Road, including the impressive Parks-Archer double barn, which is two Colony barns butted end to end. A small but vibrant community has grown up around the Butte, anchored by a quaint and colorful combination store, cafe, contract post office, and gas station.

Mud Lake ~ Jim Lake

Access from Maud Road

The Mud Lake-Jim Lake area is accessed by turning off the Old Glenn Highway onto Maud Road, (when coming from Palmer it's about 2.5 miles after crossing the Matanuska River). Travel about two miles, the paved road ends in a cul-de-sac, but if you keep going, across a small creek, the road continues. After about 2.5 more miles there will be a large parking area on the right overlooking Mud Lake, also known as Maud Lake, which is a short walk down the hill. If you drive another 1.5 miles, the main road ends and a short rough road leads to the right, down to Jim Lake. There are canoe and small boat launch sites at both lakes. This is a diverse area of interconnected lakes and streams, high on on the north side of the Knik River.

Bird-watching

This is a popular bird-watching area, as the south-facing slope often provides the only ice-free area for early arriving and late departing swans and other migratory waterfowl. The area provides nesting and/or migratory staging habitat for over 20 species of waterfowl, a wide variety of woodland songbirds, upland gamebirds, and miscellaneous raptors. The Jim Lake area has been designated an Important Bird Area of state significance by the International BirdLife and National Audubon societies, as several species have been identified which are difficult to find in other areas, such as the Sparrow, Townsend's Warbler, American Kestrel and Hammond's Flycatcher. Some species that occur regularly have special conservation status, including the Trumpeter Swan, Rusty Blackbird, Townsend's Warbler, Olive-sided Flycatcher, White-winged Crossbill and Blackpoll Warbler.

Clark-Wolverine Roads

The Clark-Wolverine area lies on the western flank of Lazy mountain, wrapped by a large sweeping bend of the Matanuska River. It's a rugged section of land, with broad hayfields falling away into steep-walled canyons. Wolverine Creek rushes across the northern part, and smaller creeks also slice through the land.

Wolverine Farm

Wolverine Farm, homesteaded by Ralph and Maxine DeVilbiss in 1956, is renowned for its fresh produce and hardy Galloway cattle. In her book titled *'Homesteading in Alaska, the Story of Wolverine Farm,'* Maxine DeVlbiss describes her first sighting of what would become her family's permanent home: "As we neared Palmer, coming up the hill from Moose Creek Camp, Ralph pulled over on the shoulder of the road, pointed across the Matanuska River, and said 'Well, Mom, there is our farm.' "A very beautiful spot, for sure, surrounded by mountains, perched on the cliffs above the river."

Little Pitchfork Ranch

In 1950, as 19-year-old Jack Seemann was helping a fellow railroad worker build a cabin and clear a garden patch, he found that he liked the area well enough to start his own place, clearing the land by hand and harvesting timber to build a home, and over the years his hard work has grown into the 600-acre Little Pitchfork Ranch, still owned and operated by Jack's descendants. Originally raising cattle, grain, and hay, the ranch now raises exotic wild game, bison and elk, in addition to hay.

Wolverine Lake

There is a good-sized lake near the end of Wolverine Road, and there is a public access road to it, but reports have been it's blocked by fallen trees and is only walk-in accessible. There is a large marshy area at the north end of the lake where the public access road ends, so waterproof boots are well-advised.

Lazy Mountain

Trails - and a Fine Vantage Point

There are delightful trails on Lazy Mountain (the peak in the photo above), and a well-marked and informative trailhead with a very nice picnic area and a sweeping view of the Matanuska Valley. Take Clark-Wolverine Road off the Old Glenn Highway, about two miles east of Palmer, and at the T intersection at the top of the first hill, take a right onto Huntley Road (photo at right). The trailhead is near the top of the long hill, watch for signs.

The steep and challenging Lazy Mountain Trail, which ascends its namesake, and the Morgan Horse Trail, which is actually an old road, both leave from this trailhead. The Morgan Horse Trail connects with the McRoberts Creek Trail, which climbs to the summit of Matanuska Peak (McRoberts Creek Trail is also accessible at the end of Smith Road). Opposite page: The view from upper Huntley Road.

Moose Creek

Fossils and Moose Range

Moose Creek tumbles out of the Talkeetna Mountains about six miles north and east of Palmer, rushes across a broad valley and through Tsadaka Canyon, where fossils of leaves and ferns can easily be found in the ancient shale.

Moose Creek is part of the 130,000 acre Matanuska Valley State Moose Range, created by the Alaska State Legislature in 1984 to maintain, improve, and enhance moose populations and habitat and other wildlife resources of the area, and to perpetuate public multiple use of the area.

Moose Creek also offers a several mile run of Class III and IV kayaking between the put-in at the end of Buffalo Mine Road and the take-out at the Moose Creek State Campground at mile 60 on the Glenn Highway.

Jonesville Mine

Evan Jones Coal Company

In 1920 a Welsh immigrant named Evan Jones, along with Anchorage pioneers Z. J. Loussac, Oscar Anderson, and three others, leased 2,240 acres on the south slope of Wishbone Hill, north of Sutton. Evan Jones had extensive mining experience in Canada and the U.S., and he organized the Evan Jones Coal Company, a privately owned mine.

The Jonesville Mine, as it came to be known, quickly developed into the largest coal mine in Alaska, supplying Anchorage, Fort Richardson and the Alaska Railroad with a high-quality coal at a time when practically all of Alaska was run by coal. In 1937 an explosion at the mine killed 14 miners and heavily damaged the mine. In the 1940's the mine couldn't hire enough miners to keep up with the demand, so the army sent men to work the mines.Between 1920 and 1968 the   Jonesville Mine produced over five million tons of coal. Mining was suspended in 1968 when the mine's primary customers, military and civilian power plants in the Anchorage area, switched from coal to natural gas. Today, due to still-active fires in the tailings, parts of the mine are under active reclamation under the Abandoned Mine Reclamation Act.

The town of Sutton, at about mile 60 of the Glenn Highway, is the location of the Jonesville Mine Road, which leads to a great area for fossil hunting. At mile 61.6, the Alpine Historical Park provides a look at the heritage and cultures of the Sutton and Chickaloon areas, including the history of the coal mining industry. Admission is free, and there is a nicely maintained park with a playground. Photo notes page 136.

CHICKALOON COAL MINES.

A.E.C.
G-1639½

Chickaloon

The Ahtna name for Chickaloon Native Village is Nay'dini'aa Na,' which means "the river with the two logs across it." The Ahtna Athabascan Tribe has occupied one of the most picturesque areas in Southcentral Alaska for 10,000 years, but as the traditional lands were subjected to mining, logging, and oil and gas drilling, the introduction of alcohol and diseases such as polio, tuberculosis, and the Spanish Influenza, brought in with development, almost wiped out the Tribe. During the 1930s-1950s, a mandatory education system intended to assimilate Alaska Natives, established and enforced by the United States government, removed many children from their families and placed them in boarding schools throughout the state. Yet through it all, the Chickaloon Tribe has endured. With the passing of the Alaska Native Claims and Settlement Act (ANCSA) of 1971, Tribal Elders re-established the Chickaloon Village Traditional Council (CVTC) in 1973, to reassert the Tribe's identity, cultural traditions, economic self-sufficiency and to reunify its citizens.

Matanuska Glacier

The Matanuska Glacier is a 27-mile long, 4-mile wide river of ice that winds out of the Chugach Mountains east of Palmer, its terminus being the source of the Matanuska River. As the largest car-accessible glacier in the state, easily visible from the Glenn Highway between milepost 100 and 110, it is perhaps also the most photographed and familiar glacier in Alaska, and is part of the great Columbia Icefield. Having once filled the entire valley of the current Matanuska River, joining with the Knik Glacier near Palmer to carve the Matanuska Valley, the glacier began ro retreat to its present location about 10,000 years ago. At milepost marker 101, you will find the Matanuska Glacier State Recreation Area, with picnic shelters, telescopes, a nature trail and a camping area. At milepost 102 a side road leads to Matanuska Glacier Park, privately owned, but the glaciers only access point. An entrance fee allows travelers to drive close to the glacier for exploring it on their own or with one of the several local guide companies who have appropriate gear to get to some of the glacier's most spectacular sites.

Part Three ~ North

Little Susitna River to the Willow Fishhook Road

The Talkeetna Mountains define the northern boundary of the Matanuska Valley. The jagged easternmost peaks provide an easy reference point from many parts of the Valley, and are complemented by the long sloping ridges dropping off to the west.

The photo above was taken on the Hatcher Pass Road. The road is maintained and kept open during the winter months to the lower parking lot of Independence Mine; the road over the pass to the Willow side closes with the first heavy snows of the season and often doesn't reopen until late June or early July. .

On the opposite page is a view from near Independence Mine, of the southeastern part of the Valley, with Bodenburg Butte at the base of Pioneer Peak; the Knik River flows between the two.

Little Susitna River ~ North

The Little Susitna River - the name means "sandy river" in the Dena'ina language - is a powerful mountain stream which begins at the Gold Mint Glacier on the flanks of Montana Peak, deep in the Talkeetna Mountains. Although not as wide nor as impressive as the Knik River or the Matanuska, the Little Su, as it's known locally, is still one of the three major rivers in the Matanuska Valley.

In 1988 the Alaska State Legislature recognized the exceptional outdoor recreational values along six southcentral Alaskan streams. The Little Susitna River is one of the designees, along with Moose Creek, Kroto Creek, the Talkeetna River, Talachulitna River, Lake Creek, and Alexander Creek. Moose Creek is the only other one in the Matanuska Valley.

A cautionary sign at the entrance to the Hatcher Pass Recreation Area warns unwary visitors of the river's dangerous force: "Admire it's power and beauty, but do not let it sweep you off your feet. Some people try their hand at recreational gold panning and an adventurous few kayak. Exercise caution; although it cannot move the largest boulders, the Little Su can easily sweep you away."

Descending rapidly down the mountain, the river slows considerably when it reaches the valley floor, becoming a pleasantly meandering river, a favorite with local fishermen.

The Willow Creek Mining District included the headwaters of the Little Su River, and placer claims were staked on all its tributaries, including Reed Creek, Archangel and Fairangel Creeks, Hatcher Creek, and Fishhook Creek.

Gold Mint Trail

Trailhead

The Hatcher Pass Recreation Area provides many spectacular routes to its mountain wilderness, and a favorite with many, from serious hikers to casual strollers, is the beautiful Gold Mint Trail at mile 13.7 of the Hatcher Pass Road. A broad paved parking area signals the trailhead, with picnic tables, interpretive signs, and restrooms. There are ten campsites/RV parking spots available, and a daily parking fee is imposed at the trailhead parking lot. While best known for the popular Gold Mint Trail, the parking area actually provides year-round opportunities for many activities. During summer months, hiking and berry-picking are popular, while in the winter months, the parking lot is used by cross-country skiers and snowshoers, and by snowmobilers to access the Hatcher Pass Snowmobile Corridor trail to Hatcher Pass via Archangel Road.

Gold Mint Trail

The views of the surrounding peaks can be spectacular at any time of the year, but especially when the varied colors of autumn paint the hillsides. The Little Susitna River rushes by the parking area, and the trail leaves from the far end of the parking lot. A relatively easy hike in its lower elevations, the Gold Mint Trail follows the Little Susitna River for eight miles, to its glacial source in the beautiful Mint Glacier Valley.

While most of the trail is easily walked, with views of the glaciers and waterfalls at the head of the valley starting about halfway in, there is a gradual gain in elevation until the last half mile, where the trail climbs steeply to provide a spectacular view of the Little Susitna River valley.

Archangel Valley

One of the most interesting valleys in the Hatcher Pass Recreation Area is Archangel Valley, site of the Fern Mine and other early prospecting remnants. Leaving the Hatcher Pass Road just above the Gold Mint parking area, the three-mile dead-end road can be rough and almost impassable at times, but the views from the end of the valley are spectacular and the blueberry picking is unequalled.

The road follows Archangel Creek up the valley, and beaver dams, ponds, and stick lodges are close to the road, as are old abandoned buildings from the mining era. There is a large boulder field at the head of the valley, providing some unique exploring, and the impressive rock faces around the valley offer challenging technical climbs for area mountaineers and rock climbers. *Photos of Archangel Valley by Bill Fikes.*

Alaskan Wildflowers

The Hatcher Pass Recreation Area offers a variety of Alaskan wildflowers, from showy blooms along the River to the tiny alpine tundra flowers found at the highest elevations.

Above: Fireweed is common along roads and trails, especially where recent fires or clearing has taken place. Several parts of the plant are edible.

Right: The wild geranium, long known as a useful medicinal plant, derives its name from a Greek word meaning 'crane.'

Opposite: The Monkshood (*Aconitum delphinifolium*) which blooms in June and early July, is one of the most toxic plants known to man. Attaining a height of three feet, with intensely blueish purple or indigo blooms, its powerful poisons were used by the Aleuts to hunt whales with poison-tipped spears. Also known as wolf's bane as its toxins were used to kill wolves. Handle with care.

Independence Mine

Robert Lee Hatcher

In the fall of 1906, Robert Lee Hatcher discovered the first lode gold claim in the Willow Creek Valley, and his claim was followed by other prospects over the next few years. Lode mining, unlike placer mining, required elaborate tunnels and heavy equipment to reach the gold-bearing ore, so the individuals who made the discoveries merged into mining companies in order to pool their resources and reduce the expenses of mining.

The Alaska Free Gold Mine on Skyscraper Mountain, and Independence Mine on Granite Mountain, were two such discoveries which merged into what is now known as the Independence Mine. In 1938 the two claims were brought together under the Alaska-Pacific Consolidated Mining Company, which became the largest gold producer in the Willow Creek Mining District, with claims covering more than 1,350 acres.

34,416 Ounces of Gold

In 1941, the peak year for production, the mine employed over 200 men and produced 34,416 ounces of gold worth $1,204,560 ($17,208,000 at today's gold prices). Twenty-two families lived in nearby Boomtown, sending eight children to the Territorial school in the bunkhouse. Buildings in the mine complex included two huge bunkhouses, an apartment house, the mine manager's house, a mess hall, plumbing shop, sheet metal shop, electrical shop, a commissary, warehouse, assay office and more. In 1942, the War Production Board designated gold mining as nonessential to the war effort and gold mining throughout the United States came to a stop. With a few notable exceptions, the mines closed. Photos courtesy of June Price, Husky Productions.

Summit Lake

A Cirque Lake

Beautiful turquoise-colored Summit Lake, located at mile 19 of the Hatcher Pass Road, is a small cirque lake, or tarn, reaching a depth of 20 feet. The surrounding terrain is all glacially carved, and this cirque was the beginning of an alpine glacier which has long since disappeared. There is a trail around the lake and along the bluff above the lake, with outstanding views to the west including the Willow Creek Drainage, the Susitna Valley, and the western arc of the Alaska Range. This scenic viewpoint is a popular picnic stop, and a launch site for paragliders in the summer, and the nearby slopes are covered with blueberries in the fall. At the southwest corner of the lake a picturesque small stream cascades down a rocky canyon.

April Bowl

April Bowl is a small high valley with another cirque lake and several ponds, accessible via a steep, narrow, half-mile long switchback trail which climbs toward Hatch Peak, east of Summit Lake. The prominent mountain to the north of this area, on the right side of the pass going west, is Skyscraper Mountain, elevation 4,775 feet. To the south is Bald Mountain Ridge, elevation 4,811 feet.

Winter Recreation

Winter recreation at the Summit Lake State Recreation Site includes snowshoeing, back country skiing, and snowboarding. The park is open to snowmachines when there is sufficient snow depth, but avalanches occur regularly on the steep slopes in the area; please use extreme caution in the winter months within the Hatcher Pass Recreation Area and the mountainous backcountry.

Willow Creek Mining District

The *Seward Weekly Gateway* reported in its July 3, 1909 edition: "Miners are jubilant at the prospects obtained. There is every indication at this time that the greatest free gold quartz camp of Alaska will center around the Willow Creek section. Prospectors, hearing the news from afar, are rushing to the scene, and the hills are fast becoming populated by gold hunters. Excitement in the quest for rich veins is intense, as it is realized that discovery of a vein means a fortune."

Several years later the gold fever still had not abated, as the *Anchorage Daily Times* reported in an article dated June 5, 1917: "...Roadhouses in the Vicinity are full up with prospectors waiting for the snow to melt so they can scour the hills."

The Willow Creek Mining District is notable as the second largest historic lode gold producer in Alaska (after Juneau). In 1897 miners discovered the first placer gold on Willow Creek, but it was several years before prospector Robert Hatcher discovered and staked the first lode gold claim in the Willow Creek valley, in 1906. The first lode mill in the area started operating two years later, in 1908, and by 1950 the Willow Creek district alone had produced 5% of Alaska's lode gold.

By 1954, Willow Creek was Alaska's largest gold mining district, with a total production approaching 18 million dollars. The Willow Creek Mining District includes the Lucky Shot mine, War Baby, Coleman, Gold Bullion, Murphy, Gold Top, and several other working mines and prospects. The historic Willow Creek Mining District also included the hardrock lode claims and placer claims on the headwaters of the Little Susitna River and its many tributary creeks.

Hatcher Pass Road

The 49-mile Hatcher Pass Road travels through only a small part of the 300,000 acre Hatcher Pass Management Area in the Talkeetna Mountains. Access from the east is via the Palmer-Fishhook Road, and access to the west side is via the Willow-Fishhook Road, mile 70 on the Parks Highway, at Willow. The road is a popular loop trip in summer, but deep snows close the summit pass in winter.

Rough Road, Hairpin Turns

From the Palmer end the road is paved all the way to Independence Mine State Historical Park, at mile 17. The west end, which climbs to Hatcher Pass Summit at 3,886 feet and drops steeply down into the Willow Creek Valley, is primarily gravel and in places will be only improved dirt, which can sometimes make it tricky to navigate large recreational vehicles. The rough road traverses steep hillsides with tight hairpin turns, and rainy weather can quickly turn the road into a slippery proposition.

That said, the trip is spectacular! Beginning on the east side, the road follows the rushing whitewater Little Susitna River through a rock-walled canyon filled with towering cottonwood trees, and up into a lush mountain valley with ragged peaks all around. Leaving the river, the road climbs quickly above treeline and into high alpine meadows carpeted with flowers and berry bushes. Panoramic mountain views are everywhere, and side roads tempt the adventurous-minded. As the road descends toward Willow Creek on the west side, watch for numerous beaver ponds below the road, and the decaying remains of old mine workings on the hillsides.

Part Four ~ West

Wasilla Creek to Burma Road

For the purposes of this book the western edge of the Matanuska Valley is more or less defined by the Little Susitna River, from where it begins angling southward just to the east of the Nancy Lake area to its wide mouth on upper Cook Inlet, a dozen miles northwest of Anchorage.

Wasilla Creek defines the eastern side of this section, as it flows mostly down the middle of the Valley from north to south, into Knik Arm and then to Cook Inlet. Burma Road is a winding dirt and gravel road which runs from Big Lake to the Point Mackenzie Road near Goose Bay.

Big Lake, Meadow Lakes, the Museum of Alaska Transportation and Industry, Fish Creek, Wasilla Creek, Burma Road and the historic Iditarod Trail are all found in this huge part of the Matanuska Valley. The even bigger Susitna Valley is only a stone's throw away.

Wasilla Creek

"Breath of Air"

Wasilla Creek is named for Chief Wasilla, a local Dena'ina Indian chief whose name is the subject of two possible explanations. One story has it being the anglicized spelling of the chief's Russian-given name, Василий Vasilij, which corresponds to the English name Basil. Early miners used the name "Wassila Creek", and claimed the word meant "breath of air" in the local Indian dialect. Whichever is correct - and they may both be - the creek does not actually flow through the town named for it. After beginning in the far northeastern part of the Valley, Wasilla Creek crosses Palmer Fishhook Road, winds through the center of the Valley, crossing Hyer Road east of Wasilla, then turns south toward Fairview Loop Road on its way to join Palmer Slough and Knik Arm.

Five Salmon Species

Wasilla Creek is home to five species of Pacific salmon, and several organizations are working on projects to protect and restore salmon habitat in Wasilla Creek. Conservation efforts began several years ago with a project to minimize recreational impacts to fragile wetland streams, with hardened trail surfaces and five bridges installed for hikers and all-terrain vehicles on small headwater streams of Wasilla Creek.

Fermented Fish Creek

In *Shem Pete's Alaska* there is an entry about Wasilla Creek, which was known as 'Chuqilintnu' or "Fermented Fish Creek": "There was once a large village at the mouth of Wasilla Creek… where it enters Palmer Slough…In pre-contact times this village and its 'chief' were destroyed by 'medicine' sent from Eklutna."

Museum of Alaska Transportation & Industry

The Museum of Alaska Transportation and Industry (MATI) was established to give a home to the transportation and industrial remnants of the state's colorful history, and to tell the many colorful stories of the people and the machines that opened Alaska to exploration and growth.

Begun in 1967 as the "Air Progress Museum" for the Alaska Centennial Celebration, the museum moved to a corner of the Alaska State Fairgrounds in 1976. The collection of old trains, planes, tractors and other machinery continued to grow until 1992, when it moved to its present 20-acre location near the Wasilla airport.

In addition to the large indoor exhibit hall, the museum has airplanes, trains, boats, military equipment, dogsleds, an original double-sized Matanuska Colony barn, and much more on display on its parklike grounds. Open Mother's Day through Labor Day.

Meadow Lakes

The Meadow Lakes region of the Matanuska Valley is that area toward the western edge of the Valley, generally north of the Parks Highway and west of Church Road. There are dozens of lakes, of all sizes, with the major lakes being Seymour and Visnaw Lakes, with at least a dozen others being more than float plane-sized. Smaller lakes and ponds dot the region, some creek-fed, some spring-fed, and some simply surface water in the low-lying areas.

The Alaska Department of Fish and Game stocks several of the lakes in this region for sport fishing, primarily with rainbow trout, and there are are public access fishing sites and boat ramps on a few of the larger lakes.

Moose and waterfowl find the many lakes in this part of the Valley to be prime habitat, and birdwatching around the lakes can be engrossing and enjoyable. Beavers, muskrats, and many other smaller wild animals also call this beautiful area their home.

Big Lake

There's an interesting section about Big Lake in *Shem Pete's Alaska*, which details the geography of more than 700 Dena'ina place-names of the western Cook Inlet Region, based on the lifetime travels and knowledge of Shem Pete and thirty-three other Dena'ina Athabascan elders.

According to Bailey Theodore there was a village at Big Lake, once attacked by the Aleuts, where fish were caught year round: "Rich people owned it. They couldn't starve. Even in February month they got silver salmon that were dark fish but lively. And lots of trout too. They could spot the fish under the ice. In two days I once caught eighty pounds of trout..."

Today Big Lake is a destination resort area, with lakeside homes, cabins, condominiums, and elegant restaurants overlooking bays with a picturesque view of distant Denali. Known as Alaska's year-round playground, sailboats, power boats, jet skis and other watercraft ply its waters in the summertime, while during the winter a network of frozen plowed ice roads criss-crosses the lake. Winter activities include snowmobiling, dog mushing, ice fishing and world-renowned cross-country skiing.

There are two state campgrounds on the lake, with 60 campsites, multiple picnic areas with shelters, and public-access boat launches.

In 1996 a devastating fire swept through the Big Lake area, consuming 37,000 acres and 433 structures before it was contained. The community has since recovered and offers all the amenities of a small town, including a shopping center with grocery, liquor, and specialty stores, a library, post office and more.

Fish Creek

Draining from the eastern edge of Big Lake and running southeast toward Cook Inlet, Fish Creek is a 14-mile salmon thruway, giving the fish access from Knik Arm to Big Lake, Meadow Creek, and the surrounding lakes and waterways.

Traditionally known as a primary fishing ground of the native Dena'ina people, a Dena'ina winter house, known as a *nichil,* was located at the outlet of Fish Creek. The creek is still a very popular place for local fishermen to gather during the summer salmon season when the Alaska Department of Fish and Game opens the waters to dipnetting. According to the ADF&G website, a personal use permit is required (in addition to a valid fishing license), and "Personal use salmon dipnetting in Fish Creek is only opened by emergency order. There is no 'normal' season."

Burma Road

A little-known but very scenic backroad in the Matanuska Valley is the dirt and gravel improved road known locally as the Burma Road, named after the infamous 700 mile supply route built between Burma and China in 1937-38.

The route roughly parallels the south shore of Big Lake before turning south near Marion Lake and winding through almost twenty miles of hills and forests before coming out near Carpenter Lake and the northern end of the Point Mackenzie Road, which links back to the south end of Knik-Goose Bay Road.

In her book, *Big Lake Beginnings*, Laurae Fortner-Welch includes information about the blazing of Burma Road by early homesteaders but notes, "The history of the Burma Road is shrouded in stories of mythical proportions."

Iditarod Trail

The historic Iditarod Trail began in Seward, followed river valleys and old native trails through the mountains and along Turnagain Arm to Girdwood, then crossed over Crow Creek Pass in the Chugach Mountains and dropped into Eagle River Valley. From there it roughly paralleled today's Glenn Highway up the east side of Knik Arm, crossed the Knik River, and doubled back down the west side of Knik Arm to the old site of Knik, where it turned west and struck out toward the Susitna River, the Alaska Range, the Iditarod goldfields, and eventually Nome, on the Bering Sea.

Today's Iditarod Trail is famous for the 1,000-mile sled dog race named for it, as well as for shorter sled dog races which also use the trail, such as the Northern Lights 300, but the historic route is also used by snowmachiners, skiers, bicyclists with winter tread tires, and other sporting enthusiasts. Winter freight is hauled over the trail to outlying lodges and cabins, and flightseeing along the trail is popular.

The Iditarod Trail was designated a National Historic Trail in 1978, as a major route of exploration, trade, and communication. Across America, only 16 trails have been honored as National Historic Trails, and the Iditarod Trail is the only Alaskan trail in the national system. Most of the historic Iditarod Trail is located on public lands; the federal Bureau of Land Management coordinates cooperative management of the trail and is the primary contact for matters involving the entire trail.

Little Susitna River ~ South

The 110-mile long Little Susitna River originates under Mint Glacier and tumbles out of the Talkeetna Mountains as a whitewater stream, then slows to meander lazily across the Valley and into Cook Inlet nine miles west of Point Mackenzie. Along the way it is joined by Archangel Creek, Fishhook Creek, Government Creek, Swiftwater Creek, and numerous smaller streams. Rainbow trout, Dolly Varden, whitefish, burbot, and several kinds of salmon can be found in the river.

There are five bridges over the river, in order they are Fishook Road, Edgerton Parks Road, Sushanna Road, Schrock Road, and the Parks Highway. Much of the land north of the Parks Highway bridge is privately owned, while most of the land below the Parks Highway Bridge is owned by the state of Alaska. *Above: Where the Little Susitna crosses the Parks Highway. Left: Woods beyond the water. Right: Bill Fikes with two Little Susitna King salmon. Photo by Frank McAllister.*

Part Five ~ Palmer

"Alaska at its Best!"

The town of Palmer is located on the bank of the powerful Matanuska RIver, with close-up views of Pioneer Peak and the jagged Chugach Mountains to the south and east, and the Talkeetna Mountains to the north.

Founded in 1935 when the government-subsidized Matanuska Colony pioneers settled in the Valley, today's Palmer is a vibrant community and the seat of the Matanuska-Susitna Borough. From major stores to friendly bistros, the businesses of Palmer create a dynamic downtown area with tree-lined streets, parks, gardens, a museum, visitor center and library, and many historic buildings. Throughout the seasons, both indoor and open-air markets and fairs with music, food, crafts and much more are a frequent event in the old train depot and on Palmer's streets.

Palmer Visitor Center and Museum

1967 Alaska Centennial Cabin

The beautiful log cabin which houses the Palmer Visitor Center was built as a community effort for the 1967 Alaska Centennial. Inside you can learn about Ahtna Athabascan natives, explore local mining and trapping history, and discover the story of the 1935 Matanuska Colony project which brought 203 farm families to the area under President Franklin Delano Roosevelt's New Deal.

Local films and documentaries play on a large-screen TV mounted above the impressive stone fireplace. Locally produced coffee is free to visitors, and a collection of free informational pamphlets on local history and lore are also free, as well as free travel guides for all of Alaska. Maps, guidebooks, and books by local authors, as well as handicrafts and interesting gift items, are for sale. The museum also presents temporary and traveling exhibits showcasing the artwork of artists and craftsmen who live in the Valley and in other regions of Alaska.

A large portion of the two-acre site is set aside for gardens, which are quite spectacular in almost any season. Annuals, perennials, bulbs, flowering trees and bushes, berries, fruits and vegetables which grow in this northern climate are all on display in their seasons, identified and labelled for visitors. Docents roam to give tours, answer questions, and explain the interesting challenges of growing flowers and vegetables in Alaska.

Educational programs, historical tours, and a commitment to depict the region's history, exploration, settlement, agriculture, and cultural and social development make this a must stop for any area visitor.

INSPECTING PALMER'S LAUNCH. KNIK APRIL 16/07.

George Palmer

A Self-Service Store

The town of Palmer traces the origin of its name to a pioneer trader, George W. Palmer, who came to Alaska in the 1890's and, among other enterprises, hauled freight to the gold miners of the Willow Creek Mining District.

One of his earliest recorded Valley enterprises was the creation of an unmanned self-service store on the eastern bank of the Matanuska River, near the present-day town named for him. Operating on the honor system and primarily serving the Ahtna people who travelled down the Matanuska River Valley from the Copper Basin, Palmer's store provided needed goods and merchandise for the remote tribe.

Valley's First Postmaster; Sailor, Banker, Merchant

A colorful entrepreneur, George Palmer was reportedly the first white settler in the Matanuska Valley. He grew the first vegetables commercially, and became the Valley's first postmaster. He also owned a store at Knik for almost 20 years, fearlessly traveling the treacherous waters of Knik Arm and Cook Inlet in his ships to resupply his much-needed stores for the miners and other settlers.

In 1913 George Palmer purchased a schooner and made trips between San Francisco and Knik, hauling freight and merchandise for his stores. Palmer served on the board of directors for the Bank of Anchorage, helped build the first clam cannery on Cook Inlet, and opened a general store in Kenai in 1921.

George Palmer had four wives from the local Dena'ina tribe, and many children and step-children. He died in 1930, at the age of 75, and is buried in the Pioneer section of the Anchorage cemetery.

Matanuska Greenbelt

The Matanuska Greenbelt encompasses over thirty miles of non-motorized trails in the very heart of the Matanuska Valley, bordered by the Palmer-Wasilla Highway, Glenn Highway, Parks Highway, and Trunk Road. Several lakes within the area offer boating, fishing, swimming, picnicking, and ice fishing in winter.

This unique area provides unparalleled access not only to the lakes, but also to forests, overlooks, steep valleys, unusual glacial landforms, farm fields and more. Trailhead signs, entry gateposts, and interpretive aids help users learn about the many features.

The Matanuska Greenbelt Trail Association works to enhance knowledge of the area and to encourage safe, responsible use by a wide diversity, including hikers, mountain bikers, runners, bird watchers, equestrians, fishermen, cross-country skiers and more.

Colony House Museum

Irene and Oscar Beylund

The Colony House Museum, located in the historic district of Palmer at 316 E. Elmwood Avenue, features the Colony home once owned by Irene and Oscar Beylund. The Beylund home traces its history back to the 1935 Roosevelt Administration's New Deal Matanuska Colony Project resettlement program.

The Beylunds were from Wisconsin, and they drew tract number 94, which was located on Scott Road, northwest of Palmer, with a stellar view of the mountains. Of the five house plans available to the Colonists, they selected this classic frame house design. The house was restored by a group known as the Colony House Preservation Project Committee, organized in 1994 for the purpose of restoring a house from the Colony era to it's 1936-1945 appearance. In 1998 the project was turned over to Palmer Historical Society, who currently operate it as a museum. The house, its furnishings, and the adjacent outbuildings display rural life in the Matanuska Valley during the heyday of the Colony.

Colony Christmas

Although the Colony House Museum is only open during the summer months, from Mother's Day to Labor Day, an open house takes place annually just before Christmas, when the Beylund home is decorated for the season and its door welcome visitors to enjoy vintage decorations, cookies and treats, and caroling around the antique piano with friends and family. Local history books, DVDs, and booklets are for sale and proceeds go to help maintain the Colony House Museum and keep its doors open to visitors.

Musk Ox Farm

The musk ox (Ovibos moschatus, also spelled muskox and musk-ox) is an Arctic mammal noted for its thick shaggy coat and named for the strong musky odor which is used by males to attract females during mating season. Musk oxen primarily live in their native lands of the Canadian Arctic and Greenland, with small introduced populations in Sweden, Siberia, Norway, and Alaska.

Known to Alaskan Natives as "Oomingmak," which means "The Bearded One," this once-endangered animal produces an annual harvest of qiviut, the finest wool in the world, prized for making sweaters, scarves, and other items. In 1968 the Musk Ox Project began workshops teaching native Alaskan women in several villages how to knit the unique lacy pattern for qiviut garments. Within a year, a knitters' cooperative was formed- Oomingmak, Musk Ox Producers' Cooperative- and within ten more years over two hundred native women were earning some of the cash income so vital to get their families through the year.

This historic 1930s-era Colony farm is home to a growing herd of 70 musk oxen, and offers guided tours, engaging exhibits, a gift shop featuring hand-knit qiviut items, and community events throughout the year. On Archie Road, two miles north of Palmer.

Springer System

John August Springer

In October of 1914, Palmer-area pioneer John August Springer filed for homestead rights to 320 acres of benchland located on the north bank of a sweeping bend in the Matanuska River, with a commanding view of Pioneer Peak and the Knik River Valley to the south and east. Springer built a log cabin and other buildings and proved up on his land, receiving the patent in 1920. Fifteen years later, in 1935, he sold part of his homestead to the United States government for $7.50 an acre for the Matanuska Colony Project, which would bring 203 new families from the depression-era Midwest to build their own homes in the Valley.

Matanuska Colony Project

The area south of Palmer which became known as the Springer System, with it's looping roads named Inner Springer and Outer Springer, is the site of some of the richest and levelest farmland in the Matanuska Valley. Of the more than 200 farms which became the Matanuska Colony Project, for which the federal government offered financing and support, over one-quarter of them were located in the Springer area.

Today the Springer System is a network of picturesque farms which would pass for almost anywhere in the midwest if not for the towering peaks of the Chugach Range. While an ever-increasing number of farms are being subdivided for tract housing, there are still enough hayfields, pastures, croplands and massive Colony barns to give the area a friendly rural feel. At the end of E. DePriest Avenue, in the southeast corner of the Springer System, the logs of John Springer's cabin can still be seen on a bluff overlooking the Matanuska River.

Matanuska Experiment Farm

The first Alaska Agricultural Experiment Station was established in Sitka in 1898, and subsequent stations were opened at Kodiak, Kenai, Rampart, Copper Center, Fairbanks, and Matanuska. Only two of these remain, the Fairbanks Experiment Farm and the Matanuska Experiment Farm, which provides research in sustainable agriculture, land reclamation and other environmental issues. The Experiment Farm includes 800 acres of forest land and 260 acres of cultivated land, including barns, feed storage facilities and pasture land, and farm equipment to produce and harvest grain, hay, and other crops. There are also field and laboratory facilities for research on soils, plants and livestock, and an adjacent greenhouse facility, operated by the Alaska Department of Natural Resources.

Open house Agricultural Days are an annual event welcoming the public to visit.

Palmer Fishhook Road

The Palmer Fishhook Road, which runs between the Glenn Highway (just north of Palmer) and Hatcher Pass, is noted for its picturesque rural images, with pastoral scenes of horses grazing, Colony barns, and tilled fields rolling away toward the Talkeetna Mountains to the north.

While subdivisions have inevitably encroached upon the rich farmlands, much of the Palmer Fishhook Road area has maintained an idyllic midwestern feel. Bountiful gardens, including one of the Matanuska Valley's premier nurseries, attest to the superb soils found in the area. Spring Creek Farm, on Farm Loop Road, is part of Alaska Pacific University's 750-acre Kellogg Campus, and operates a productive ecologically and sustainably managed vegetable farm, selling produce via its CSA (community supported agriculture) program, in which members sign up for shares weekly throughout the growing season.

Alaska State Fair

For two weeks at the end of every Alaskan summer the Alaska State Fair offers a heady experience for residents and visitors alike, with its famous giant vegetables, local livestock and produce, beautiful flower gardens, world-class entertainers, and favorite foods such as salmon quesadillas and Denali cream puffs. Labeled the 'Last Blast of Summer,' the Alaska State Fair delivers a thrilling showcase of Alaska's beauty and uniqueness.

The Matanuska Valley Fair Association was formed in July 1936, and the first event took place that September. It was a four-day Fair, held on the school grounds, now the Mat-Su Borough offices. The inaugural event coincided with the opening of the Knik River Bridge, which linked the city of Anchorage and the Valley by road for the first time. That first year's events included the crowning of the Fair queen, a baby show, boxing matches, horse races, dances, a rodeo and baseball games. There were also hundreds of agricultural entries, including giant cabbages, grain, carrots, onions, celery, peas and other vegetables.

The Fair has grown and expanded since the first event in 1936, but the spirit of the Fair remains the same, and the heart of the Fair still centers on the things the original Colonists started with: agriculture, produce, lots of food, flowers, friends and family, and an old-fashioned good time. The Alaska State Fair offers year-round services, including horse shows, facility rentals, concerts, and winter RV & boat storage. From weddings in the historic Colony Church to major trade shows in Raven Hall, the Fair hosts events on a continuing basis.

Part Six ~ Wasilla

"Home of the Iditarod"

In the spring of 1916, when the government railroad crossed the old Carle Wagon Road which rand between the town of Knik and the Willow Creek Mining District at Hatcher Pass, a railroad construction camp was built, and by the following summer a townsite had been surveyed, staked, streets laid out and fifty lots had been sold.

As the closest town to the Willow Creek and Hatcher Pass mining areas, Wasilla became the shipping point for the gold concentrates. By 1935 Wasilla was the largest town in the Matanuska Valley, with a population of approximately 100 people.

Today Wasilla is still the largest town in the Valley, and the sixth-largest city in Alaska, with the 2010 population at 7,831. It is the commercial hub of the Matanuska-Susitna Borough, and for several years has consistently been listed as one of the fastest-growing cities in the United States.

Wasilla Lake

The 1910 Sleem map of the Willow Creek Mining District shows the Chickaloon Trail, the primary east-west route through the Valley, passing along the south shore of Wasilla Lake and the north shores of Cottonwood and Finger Lakes, through an area the Dena'ina called *Benteh*, meaning 'among the lakes'.

In *Shem Pete's Alaska* Wasilla lake is identified as *Lach Bena*, meaning 'Silt (Mud) Lake,' and area historian Heinie Snider is quoted: "Fishermen who have fished in Wasilla Lake know that there is more than one lake and there are at least three good lakes–connected to each other by a small stream. Between lake number one and number two, some time ago there stood some old buildings–known to the old-timers as the Wasilla cabins. Old Chief Vasili's grave was there..."

Today Wasilla Lake is the centerpiece of the town named for it, with beaches which become a gathering place for local families on hot summer days. Powerboats, sailboats, canoes and other watercraft frequent the lake, and floatplanes arrive and take off almost daily.

Dorothy Page Museum

The beautiful log building which houses the museum, now a National Historic Landmark, was built in 1931 as a community hall for the Wasilla area. In 1967, during the Alaska Centennial, the building was refurbished to become Wasilla's first museum, and in 1978 it became the first headquarters for the Iditarod Trail Sled Dog Race Committee.

Today the museum showcases the history of the Wasilla area with a fine collection of relics, artifacts, and what were once everyday useful items to the pioneers who settled the Valley. Displays include a diorama of early-day Wasilla, an assemblage of unique utensils and items which an early homesteader would have used, taxidermy mounts of area wildlife, and a display of tools and items from the Willow Creek Mining District. The museum sponsors programs and lectures which interpret and explain important points in area history, and the museum also maintains the Historic Town Site Park.

Wasilla Townsite Park

When early historians of the Wasilla area realized how much of the town's history was being lost to development, they made a wise effort to preserve several significant structures, including the Herning-Teeland-Mead house (1936), the area's first schoolhouse (1917), prospector Paddy Marion's cabin, Shorty Gustafson's barn, Nels Larson's blacksmith shop, a sauna bath-house and the Capitol Site log cabin (photo page 115).

The Capitol Site cabin was built when the people of Alaska voted to move the Capitol from Juneau to Willow in the early 1970's and then-Governor Jay Hammond stated that he would move into a tent at the new Capitol site. Enough people thought a more appropriate structure should be provided that a fund-raising effort was undertaken and what would be the first structure on the new Capitol site was built, but the legislature never appropriated the funding for the actual move.

Wasilla Depot ~ Alaska Railroad

National Register of Historic Places

The historic Alaska Railroad depot in Wasilla, built in 1916-17 and listed on the National Register of Historic Places, is where the train stops to pick up passengers on its travels between Seward and Fairbanks and other points along the tracks, however the building is not staffed by the Alaska Railroad. The building owned by the federal government, but is leased to the Wasilla Chamber of Commerce for their meetings, and the building is often closed and locked at train arrival and departure times.

Multiple Paint Jobs

The Wasilla depot has been transformed a number of times in its almost 100 year history. From 1947 to 1952 the Alaska Railroad's post-war rehabilitation program included a spruce up campaign along the entire railroad, and the Wasilla depot, like others, was painted beige with a dark brown trim on the doors, windows, frames, casements and other details. For the 1976 U.S. Bicentennial celebration the depot received a very patriotic paint job: white with red trim, and a blue line of fascia boards around the roofline. Sometime in the 1980's the depot was given it's current coat of dark forest green with white trim.

On the east side of the depot a set of historical information signs have been placed, telling the story of how the railroad bypassed the town of Knik in favor of Wasilla, and how miner Orville G. Herning became the town's leading merchant. Lamp posts reminiscent of a bygone era stand around the depot area, and during the summer months bountiful baskets of flowers hang from the depot's eaves and fill the flowerbeds alongside the tracks.

Lake Lucille

Named in 1898 by Captain Edwin F. Glenn, an explorer for the US Army, Lake Lucille is a 362 acre natural freshwater lake. The west-end outlet has a weir with a fish pass allowing fish to leave Lake Lucille and travel down Lucille Creek into Meadow Creek, and from there to Big Lake. In *Shem Pete's Alaska*, Bailey Theodore is quoted: "Our great-great-grandfather bought this lake for us people to fish in..." And Mike Theodore adds: "They paid for that lake with *k'enq'ena* [dentalia beads]."

There is a city park at the east end of the lake, and the 80-acre Lake Lucille Park on the southern shore, accessible via Knik-Goose Bay Road. Owned by the Matanuska - Susitna Borough, the park is a wooded area with a campground, fire pits, restrooms, and scenic trails, with a boardwalk along the lake.

Cottonwood Creek

A scenic waterway in the Matanuska Valley and the primary route of the Seven Mile Canoe Trail, Cottonwood Creek begins in the central part of the Valley, near Niclason Lake, drops south and crosses Bogard Road, then skirts the edge of Finger Lake and runs into the east end of Cottonwood Lake, which is one of the chain of lakes crossing the middle of the Valley.

From the west end of Cottonwood Lake it drains into Mud Lake, then becomes a creek again for a short ways before emptying into upper Wasilla Lake and finding an outlet in the corner of lower Wasilla Lake. From there it crosses the Parks Highway and winds through forests and suburban backyards all the way to the bluffs of Cook Inlet, where it cuts a serpentine path across the Inlet mud before joining Knik Arm below Settler's Bay.

Iditarod Headquarters

The Iditarod Trail Sled Dog Race, which runs from Anchorage to Nome every March, is the most popular sporting event in Alaska. Teams come from all over the world to compete in the 1,000 mile race across western Alaska, through vast forests, across frozen lakes and rivers, over numerous mountain ranges, and along the shores of the Bering Sea. Begun in 1973 by visionary musher Joe Redington, Sr., the Iditarod, as it's widely known, is among the toughest endurance events in the world, and just finishing the race is a major accomplishment; in 41 years there have only been 21 Iditarod champions.

The headquarters of the Iditarod Trail Sled Dog Race is a log cabin two miles south of Wasilla, on Knik Goose Bay Road, built in 1986. Tucked among towering spruce trees, with a large lawn and plenty of flowers in the summer, the headquarters cabin features a small museum with historical displays, impressive trophies, video exhibits, portraits of past champions, and antique race paraphernalia on display.

Sled dog rides are available in the summer months, and the driver, Raymie Redington, is a 10-time race finisher and the son of race founder Joe Redington, Sr. A replica of the checkpoint cabin at Rohn, mile 188 on the Iditarod Trail, is a popular stop, as are life-size statues of Joe Redington and his favorite lead dog, and a replica of the historic bronze statue of Balto which stands in New York's Central Park. The original was a tribute to the dogs of the 1925 Serum Run, which saved Nome from a diphtheria epidemic.

Teelands Country Store

The Beginnings of Wasilla

Wasilla came into existence at the intersection of the old Carle Wagon Road and the government railroad which was being constructed from Anchorage to Fairbanks. A railroad construction camp was built on the site in the spring of 1916, and by the following summer fifty townsite lots had been sold. A store owner from Knik, Orville G. Herning, purchased three of the townsite lots and built a 24' x 80' store, the first permanent building in the new town of Wasilla, which he operated until his death in 1947.

Walt and Vi Teeland

Upon Herning's death the store and his home, located behind the atore, were purchased by Walter and Vivian Teeland, who operated it as Teeland's Country Store until 1972, when they retired. For many decades the Teeland's Country Store was a landmark in the Matanuska Valley, sitting at the intersection of Wasilla's Main Street and the Parks Highway, directly across from the Wasilla depot of the Alaska Railroad. Walt and Vi, as they were known, operated the store as a combination grocery, general goods, and hardware store, and it was the only business of its kind between Palmer and Willow. For many years the Iditarod Trail Sled Dog Race had its headquarters on the second floor, moving to their present location on Knik-Goose Bay Road in 1986.

When the Teelands retired, the store was purchased by Jules Mead and eventually donated to the city of Wasilla. In 1987 the store was moved two blocks north to accommodate widening of the Parks Highway. Today the building is a popular sandwich shop/bistro and is listed on the National Register of Historic Places.

Seven Mile Canoe Trail

This seven mile canoe or kayak journey begins at Finger Lake and ends at Wasilla Lake, winding westward through the lakes and along Cottonwood Creek from Finger Lake to Cottonwood Lake, then to Mud Lake and finally to Wasilla Lake, with a short portage between Finger Lake and Cottonwood Lake. There are sloping docks at either end of the portage, making the exit and reentry a simple matter.

Most the of shoreline around the lakes is private property, but there are plenty of wild areas to explore, and wildlife in the lakes includes assorted waterfowl, muskrats, and an occasional moose. Chinook salmon, Rainbow Trout, Arctic char, Arctic grayling, and other species of sport fish are stocked in Finger Lake and present in the other lakes along the canoe trail. Alaska fishing license required; be familiar with the regulations.

Valley Resources

Mat-Su Visitors Center
Mile 35.5 Parks Highway
www.alaskavisit.com
907-746-5000

Dorothy Page Museum
323 North Main St., Wasilla.
Open all year. 907-373-9071
www.cityofwasilla.com/museum

Palmer Visitors Center
723 South Valley Way, Palmer
907-745-8878
www.palmermuseum.org

Colony House Museum
316 E. Elmwood Avenue, Palmer
Open May-August. 907-746-1935
www.palmerhistoricalsociety.org

Museum of Alaska Transportation & Industry
Mile 47, Parks Highway, 3800 W.
Museum Dr., 907-376-1211

Iditarod Trail
www.blm.gov/ak/st/en/prog/nlcs/
iditarod.html

Iditarod Headquarters
Mile 2.2 Knik-Goose Bay Road,
Wasilla. Open all year.
907-376-5155 www.iditarod.com

Wasilla Townsite
At the corner of Boundary and
Swanson Streets, Wasilla.
907-376-2005
www.wkhsociety.org

Knik Museum, Mushers Hall
Mile 13.9 Knik-Goose Bay Rd,
open May-Sept, Thursdays
through Sundays 1-6 pm.
907-376-7755

Musk Ox Farm
Mile 50 Glenn Highway, 12850
Archie Road, Palmer.
907-745-4151
www.muskoxfarm.org

Independence Mine
Mile 18 Hatcher Pass Road, open
June-Sept, guided tours available
in summer. 907-745-2827

Matanuska Greenbelt Trails
Landholders cooperative
www.matanuska-greenbelt.org

Alaska State Fair
2075 Glenn Highway, Palmer
www.alaskastatefair.org

Palmer Hay Flats
http://www.palmerhayflats.org

Knik
freepages.genealogy.rootsweb.anc
estry.com/~coleen/knik.html

Jonesville Mine
http://alaskamininghalloffame.org/
inductees/jones.php •
stanstark.blogspot.com/2011/08/
jonesville-mine-palmer-alaska.html

Hatcher Pass Recreation Area
http://dnr.alaska.gov/parks/units/
hatcherpass/hatcherpass.htm

George W. Palmer
freepages.genealogy.rootsweb.anc
estry.com/~coleen/gwp.html

Matanuska Glacier
www.matanuska-glacier.com

Bodenburg Butte
haktrailhead.com/bodenburg/
bodenburg.shtml

Recommended Reading

The Matanuska Colony Barns: The Enduring Legacy of the 1935 Matanuska Colony Project, by Helen Hegener, Northern Light Media, 2013
matanuskabarns.wordpress.com

Shem Pete's Alaska: The Territory of the Upper Cook Inlet Dena'ina James Kari and James A. Fall, Principal Contributor Shem Pete, 1987, 2003, University of Alaska Press

Early Days in Wasilla, by Louise Potter, Hanover, 1963, reprinted in 2002 by Alaskana Books, Palmer

Matanuska Valley Memoir: The Story of How One Alaskan Community Developed, by Hugh A. Johnson and Keith L. Stanton, Alaska Experiment Station, 1955

The First Summer: Photographs of the Matanuska Colony of 1935, by James H. Fox, A.R.R.C., 1980

We Shall Be Remembered, Evangeline Atwood, Alaska Methodist University, 1966

The Colorful Matanuska Valley, Don L. Irwin, 1968

Alaska's Farms and Gardens, Alaska Geographic Vol. 11, No. 2 Frontier Physician: The Life and Legacy of Dr. C. Earl Albrecht, by Nancy Jordan, Epicenter Press, 1995

The Matanuska Colony: 75th Anniversary Scrapbook, by Lorraine M. Kirker and Lynette A. Lehn, Alaskana Books, 2010

The Matanuska Colony: Fifty Years 1935-1985, by Bridgette Lively, Matanuska Impressions Printing, 1985

Old Times on Upper Cook's Inlet, by Louise Potter, Book Cache, 1967

The Frontier In Alaska and the Matanuska Colony, by Orlando W. Miller, Yale University Press, 1975

Knik, Matanuska, Susitna: A Visual History of the Valleys, by Vickie Cole et al, printed by Matanuska-Susitna Borough, L&B Printing, 1985

Buildings of Alaska, Alison K. Hoagland Oxford University Press, 1993

Big Lake, Alaska: Beginnings, by Laurae Fortner-Welch, Big Lake Library Advocates, 1992
Homesteading in Alaska, Story of Wolverine Farm, by Maxine DeVilbiss, 2003

Independence Mine and the Willow Creek Mining District, by Kathryn Koutsky Cohen, State of Alaska Dept. of Natural Resources, Office of History/Archeology 1982

A Walk-About Guide to Alaska, Volume Three: Palmer Area & Hatcher Pass, by Shawn Lyons, Shawn R. Lyons, 2001

MATANUSKA-SUSITNA VALLEY, ALASKA , Researching Our South Central Alaska Roots, by Coleen Mielke 2013
freepages.genealogy.rootsweb.anc estry.com/%7Ecoleen/ south_central_alaska.html

LitSite Alaska: The Matanuska Valley Colony, online at http:// www.litsite.org/index.cfm? section=Digital-Archives&page=Industry&cat=Agri culture&viewpost=2&ContentId=27 52

Photo Index

Book Index

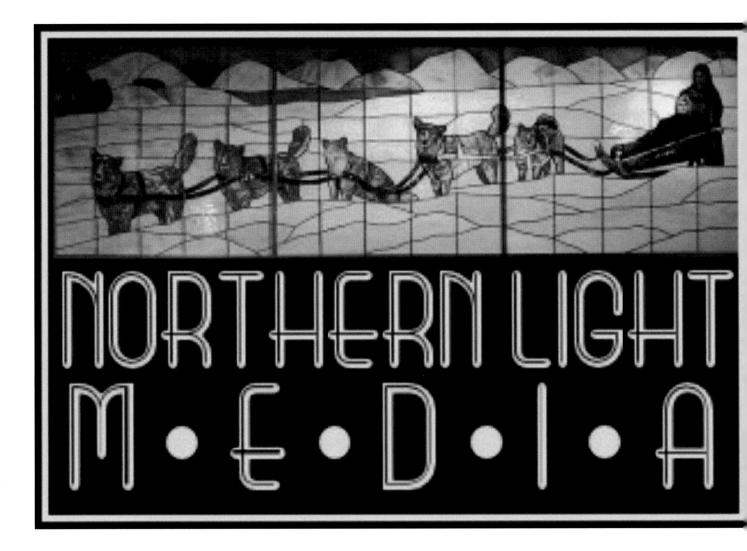

Also from Northern Light Media

Northern Light Media is an Alaskan company, founded in 2007 and owned by Helen Hegener, which publishes books and produces documentary videos about Alaska and Alaskan subjects.

Northern Light Media has also produced two popular and well-attended Mushing History Conferences; and is an active supporter of the Northern Lights 300 Sled Dog Race, run in January, on the Iditarod Trail.

northernlightmedia.wordpress.com

THE MATANUSKA COLONY BARNS

The Matanuska Colony Barns details the history of these magnificent reminders of the 1935 Matanuska Colony Project. From the back cover: "Anyone who travels through the eastern part of Alaska's dramatically beautiful Matanuska Valley soon finds a Colony barn enhancing the landscape."

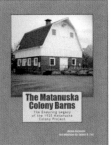

The Matanuska Colony Barns: The Enduring Legacy of the 1935 Matanuska Colony Project, by Helen Hegener, photographs by Eric Vercammen and others. Introduction by James H. Fox. 140 pages, full color. ISBN 978-0-9843977-4-7.
Includes maps, index, bibliography, resources.

matanuskabarns.wordpress.com

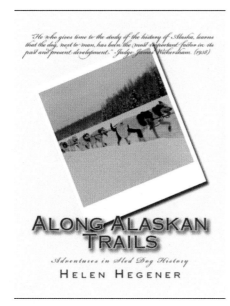

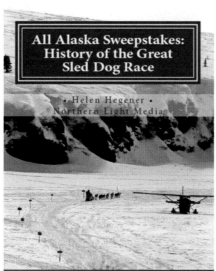

Along Alaskan Trails

A collection of true stories about Alaskan sled dogs and the role they played in the development of the north, with dozens of historic photos from the archives of the Alaska State Library, the University of Alaska Fairbanks, and other sources. In every part of this great land, from the misty fjords of southeastern Alaska to the farthest northern tip of the continent, sled dogs were the most dependable – and often the only – form of transportation. The dog team made travel and moving loads over otherwise impassable trails possible. **Along Alaskan Trails, Adventures in Sled Dog History**, by Helen Hegener. Published in July, 2012.

alongalaskantrails.wordpress.com

The All Alaska Sweepstakes

With colorful drivers like "Scotty" Allan and Leonhard Seppala, who each won the race three times, the All Alaska Sweepstakes was an eagerly anticipated annual event. In 1983 the Nome Kennel Club sponsored the 75th Anniversary race, and Rick Swenson took home the $25,000.00 purse.

Then, in 2008, for the 100th Anniversary of the event, the Nome Kennel Club offered the richest purse ever for a sled dog race: $100,000.00 winner-take-all, and mushers from all across the state signed on for the historic race to Candle and back. Published in 2013. 160 pages, over 350 photos.

allalaskasweepstakes.wordpress

Appetite & Attitude

Lance Mackey is the world's preeminent long distance sled dog racer. He made racing history when he won two 1,000 mile races back-to-back, the Yukon Quest and the Iditarod, with most of the same dogs – an incredible feat of endurance, long considered almost impossible, which changed how mushers think about what their dogs are capable of achieving.

Lance then went on to win both races a total of four times each, including an unprecedented four straight Iditarod wins. He is one of the greatest mushers who ever lived. In this 45-minute video Lance talks about his races, his dogs, and the roots of his mushing history.

northernlightmedia.com/?p=36

Made in the USA
Las Vegas, NV
23 December 2021